SECRET HOUR

Jenny Stafford

BROADWAY PLAY PUBLISHING INC
New York
www.broadwayplaypublishing.com
info@broadwayplaypublishing.com

SECRET HOUR
© Copyright 2023 Jenny Stafford

Cover art: DALL-E

First edition: March 2023
I S B N: 978-0-88145-972-2

Book design: Marie Donovan
Page make-up: Adobe InDesign
Typeface: Palatino

SECRET HOUR received its world premiere production at the Capital Repertory Theatre (Artistic Director, Maggie Mancinelli-Cahill) in Albany, New York, from 27 January-19 February 2023. The cast and creative contributors were:

KATE .... Marina Shay
BEN .... Joshua David Robinson
LEAF .... Whit K Lee

Director .... Margaret E Hall
Set design .... David McQuillen Robertson
Lighting design .... Travis McHale
Costume design .... Andrea Adamczyk
Sound design .... Julian Evans

SECRET HOUR received development and support from the HBMG Foundation's National Winter Playwrights Retreat, the Butterfly Effect Theatre Company, And Toto Too Theatre, and Prologue Theatre Company.

Special thanks to Rob Hartmann and Ian Clary.

CHARACTERS & SETTING

KATE, F, 35, an Ethics professor at a university. Funny, intelligent, sure of herself.

BEN, M, 35, KATE's husband. Likable, funny. Quick, smart, impulsive. Talks before he thinks.

LEAF/DOCTOR, M, 40, a handyman. Funny, a stoner/surfer vibe, very go-with-the-flow, ethereal.

Present day, January-May. A spring semester.

A note on casting: Every effort should be made to cast with a diverse cast of actors. If LEAF is cast as an actor of color, special attention should be paid that he is not the only actor of color.

For Mark, who believed from the beginning.

Prologue

(January. KATE, *mid-30s, stands at the front of a college lecture hall. She is poised, professional, and highly entertaining. Her lecture has a slight feel of stand-up comedy to it. Throughout the play, she addresses the audience as her classroom of students.)*

KATE: Alrighty, hopefully everyone grabbed a syllabus on the way in. If you look at it, you will see that this is Introduction to Ethics. I'm sincerely hoping this is not your actual introduction to ethics—if so, I am concerned for your friends and family. But rather your introduction to the *study* of ethics, with me, Professor Gordon.

So why study ethics? I'm sure some of you are here because you heard I don't give a traditional final exam. That part is true—there is only one question on the final, and I'll tell it to you now: Is your highest ethical responsibility to yourself, or to other people? *(She scans the room and laughs.)* Oooh, some of you look nervous! And yes, you'll have to support your final answer with a theory of ethics that we study.

So let's look at two of those theories, that strive to answer your final exam for you—is your highest ethical responsibility to yourself, or to other people? Raise your hand if you think it's to yourself. *(She scans the audience.)* Does nobody think that, or you're just too scared to admit it? *(If members of the audience raise their hands, change to* "Do not more of you think that, or are you just scared to admit it?".*)* RAISE YOUR HANDS!

Ah, some brave Nietzsche souls. And how many think it's to other people? *(She scans the audience.)* Ah, the Confucians. No, not confusions. Some of you look like the confusions right now.

Yes, these are two of the philosophers we will be looking at more in depth. An epic showdown of Nietzsche vs. Confucius! *(She holds a pretend microphone and mimics a boxing announcer voice.)* In this corner, weighing in at a hundred and eighty pounds, with some questionable political leanings and a penchant for Wagner we have NEITZSCHE! He will try to convince you that you should throw off the yolk of mass culture and be true to yourself--and while Nietzsche himself didn't believe this, the bigger idea is that by elevating yourself, you elevate society as a whole. More on that later.

And in this corner, weighing in at two hundred and forty pounds, hailing from the far east with a penchant for getting exiled its CONFUSCIUUUUUUS! He will try to convince you that your highest calling is to your family and your role in society, and that by fulfilling your role well you fulfill yourself along the way. *(She drops her imaginary mic.)* We'll see who wins your heart and mind this semester. We'll meet again on Wednesday. Oh! And I forgot something very important. *(She leans forward, as if looking into each of their eyes individually.)* Do not. Lie to me. This semester. *(Beat)* If you lie to me—*your ethics professor*—and I find out about it, you will automatically fail this class. Do not pass go, do not collect two hundred dollars. And I will warn you now, the ghosts of the dishonest students who have come before you have blown your covers, and I am on to you. I know about increasing the size of the font, just on the periods, to make your paper longer. I know about changing the time zone on your computer to make the time stamp look like you submitted your paper by the deadline.

Do not. Lie to me. This semester. *(Beat)* Have a great day, I'll, see you on Wednesday!

(The scene transitions around KATE. *She stays standing center, and the elements of a middle-class home arrive onstage around her. She sits on a couch. Transition to—)*

Scene One

*(*KATE *sits on the couch looking over papers.* BEN, *her husband, walks in the front door carrying a grocery bag and a mail package, and wearing a Best Buy polo.)*

BEN: Hey, babe!

KATE: Hey! How was your day?

BEN: Amazing.

KATE: Really?

BEN: No. A guy brought his computer to the help desk today, and I was talking him through how to fix it. I said "Click 'start', then click 'my computer.'" And he said, "Oh, it isn't my computer. It's my wife's". *(He playfully falls face first onto the couch next to* KATE.) Remember when I was an engineer? Remember happiness?

*(*KATE *indicates the package.)*

KATE: What's this?

BEN: Oh! It's a rock polisher! *(He rips open the package.)* I got this book on identifying different kinds of rocks. Thought maybe I'd go hiking this weekend. See what's around here. Polish them up. Start a collection.

KATE: *(Not sure how to respond)* That sounds…great.

BEN: I mean, there's only three kinds of rocks, but there are nine different rock formations. Who knows, maybe I'll Pokemon it and find them all! How was your day?

(BEN *sits on the couch and starts massaging* KATE'*s feet.*
She indicates that he should lift his feet, and they massage
each other's feet as they talk.)

KATE: Oh my God! Remember that article I wrote last
summer? I found out it's getting published! And they
want me to present on it at a conference in Boston!
How great is that? Wanna go to Boston?

BEN: Heck yeah! Congrats!

KATE: That's going to help so much with tenure.
And the woman who runs the conference said
there's a good chance it will lead to other speaking
engagements—maybe even another book.

BEN: Well, I'd say you had a pretty good day!

KATE: That was the highlight. Other than that, you
know, first day of the semester, lots of syllabi.

BEN: Did you make anyone cry this time?

KATE: I don't make them cry! (*Beat*) Except—

BEN & KATE: —that one girl—

BEN: Lucy? Laura?

KATE: Lola. But she cried at everything! That wasn't
me!

BEN: It was a little you.

KATE: Okay, it was a *little* me. But I'm sorry, if the
syllabus makes you cry, I can't help you. And that's
what I told her. And then she cried more.

BEN: And then you told her you had to go and you left
her there!

KATE: I *did* have to go! But I told her she could come
cry during office hours the next day.

BEN: And that's why you are going to be a wonderful
and terrifying mother. (*He leans forward and kisses her.*
He reaches into the grocery sack and pulls out a pregnancy

test.) Speaking of which…it's test day! Hey-oh! Let's go!

KATE: Oh…I already took it. Before you got home.

BEN: What?!

KATE: It's like, the twentieth time, Ben. We don't have to make a production out of it every time. And I couldn't stand to see you crash into despair again.

BEN: I don't do that.

KATE: You do it every time. Sometimes it comes out in going for a run, or eating a whole cake…or both, that one really unfortunate night.

BEN: That was a long night at the ER.

KATE: But the point is, you do it. And it makes me feel awful.

(BEN *turns to* KATE *and takes her face in his hands.)*

BEN: Hey. You aren't a failure. I don't ever, ever want you to feel like that.

KATE: *(She bristles.)* I didn't say I feel like a failure.

(Beat)

BEN: You know what I mean.

KATE: Yeah.

BEN: So…it was a no?

(KATE *nods. A moment)*

BEN: See, no big deal. It's fine.

KATE: Yeah. Next month, right? Lucky try number twenty-one!

BEN: Yep. *(He pulls a full cake out of the grocery bag, and starts eating it.)*

KATE: No, no, no! This is exactly what I meant!

BEN: *(Through a mouthful of cake, spitting crumbs everywhere)* I don't get it. We got checked. My stuff works. Your stuff works. What the hell?!

KATE: You have to stop! Do you know how embarrassing it is to drive you to the hospital for cake cramps? Multiple times?

BEN: *(Still with mouthfuls of cake)* How many positions did we try? We even did that wheelbarrow one. What are we, Cirque du Soleil?!

KATE: Look, if you're gonna eat all that cake, at least share it.

(KATE reaches for BEN's fork, and he pulls it away from her. She tries again. He does it again.)

KATE: Ben, it's a full sheet cake for like twenty people. Share!

BEN: Alright, alright!

(BEN hands KATE the fork and she takes a bite of the cake.)

BEN: I started researching again. The tests we can get. Hormone shots. There's invitro.

KATE: That's all so hard on my body though, Ben. And expensive. We can't afford that.

BEN: What's the alternative? We just never have kids?

(Beat)

KATE: I mean, that was our original plan. Maybe we were right the first time. Maybe it's just not meant to be.

BEN: What did we know? We were kids ourselves. We didn't know what we wanted. Now we do. Right? We changed our minds.

KATE: Of course. Of course we did.

(BEN *and* KATE *eat cake in silence for a moment.* LEAF *enters from stage right. He is tall with a ponytail and a toolbelt, and has a kind of ethereal quality about him.*)

LEAF: I've got good news and bad news, and then some more good news.

(BEN *and* KATE *jump.*)

KATE: Leaf! Oh my god, I thought you left hours ago!

LEAF: No, I'm still here.

(Beat)

BEN: What's the news, Leaf?

LEAF: Okay, well, the good news is that it was a tiny drip. But the bad news is that you let it go long enough that it caused some big problems. I pulled out that cabinet and the carpet behind it was soaked…I think the whole floor has to be replaced in there. I can do that for you.

BEN: Oh, God. How long will that take?

LEAF: Like, a week.

KATE: You said there was more good news?

LEAF: There's a family of rabbits hopping around outside the window in there and it's adorable. *(Beat)* I'm just gonna wash my hands in the kitchen. *(He crosses and exits.)*

KATE: Honey, he's been here for weeks. It's becoming like, a hostage situation. We have to hire someone else.

BEN: No, Mark swears he's good.

KATE: Is that the guy who keeps the smelly cheese in the fridge at work?

BEN: Yeah, but he used to be a contractor. He says Leaf is good; he's just slow. And he's cheap! He's gonna fix this for way less than anyone else.

KATE: When? In a year? He's in our house every day!

BEN: Hey, you're the one who's so worried about money.

KATE: I'm not convinced he's even a certified—

(LEAF enters again, carrying a fork. He sits on the couch and takes a bite of the cake.)

LEAF: How was everyone's day?

KATE: Um…it was great. You know, Leaf, we know so little about you and you are here…so, so much. Tell us about yourself! Like…how did you get into construction?

LEAF: It's a funny story.

(Beat)

BEN: Tell it.

LEAF: Well, I took a semester off from college to go to Guatemala with Habitat for Humanity. I didn't know anything about building when I got there. But it changed my life. I built my very first house, and this little Guatemalan family stood in front of it, and looked at me and said— *(He looks out dreamily in front of him.)* "No temenos hogar, pero no viviremos aqui".

KATE: *(A little taken in)* Wow. What does that mean?

LEAF: "We are homeless, but we won't live here."

BEN: Oh…

LEAF: Humanity did not want my habitat. I decided that if I was gonna do this, I had to become like, the Lance Armstrong of construction. So I did some drugs, worked really hard, and built a lot of habitats that humanity *did* want. Then I came home, and I built the house I live in now.

KATE: Wow, really?

LEAF: Oh yeah. It's a treehouse, off Route 6.

KATE: You…live in a treehouse? As your permanent residence?

LEAF: Oh yeah. It's amazing. I'm free. Plus I'm an avid birdwatcher, so it works out great. You're just sitting there, eating dinner, and you're like— *(He looks to the left and points.)* "There's one." *(Beat)* Well, I should get going. Any other questions?

KATE: So many.

BEN: Nah, we're good. Thanks, Leaf.

LEAF: No problem at all. I'll do the dishes— *(He collects their forks.)* —and I'll see you fine folks tomorrow! *(He starts to leave, and then turns back.)* And hey you guys, don't give up on the baby thing. It's gonna happen.

(LEAF exits into the kitchen. KATE and BEN exchange a shocked look. He scoops some icing off the cake with his finger and eats it.)

Scene Two

(A month later. February. KATE and BEN's house. KATE sits on the couch with a glass of wine, reading a book. LEAF pops out from the bathroom.)

LEAF: Hey, hey!

(KATE jumps, almost choking on her wine.)

KATE: Hey, Leaf. How's the bathroom coming?

LEAF: It's getting there. I've got some good news and some bad news.

KATE: Great.

LEAF: The bad news is…I replaced all the flooring, but after I did, I noticed that the bathtub looks like it's sinking, and it turns out the flooring was rotting under the bathtub too. So I'm gonna have to pull it out and redo that flooring too.

(KATE *puts her head in her hands.*)

KATE: How long is that going to take?

LEAF & KATE: Like, a week?

KATE: Well, it's been like a month since the last time you said it would take a week.

LEAF: I don't know, man…the house tells *me* what it needs.

KATE: How much is that going to cost?

LEAF: Oh, no additional cost.

KATE: Is that the good news?

LEAF: Oh, no. The good news is I got my life coaching certification today! Done?

(LEAF *takes her empty wine glass and exits into the kitchen, then returns with a soda.* KATE *can't help herself.*)

KATE: Your what? You got your what?

LEAF: My life coaching certification!

KATE: What…what are you going to do with that?

LEAF: Coach lives.

KATE: …Why?

LEAF: I can help people with whatever they need. But my specialty is helping people break free of lives they don't want to be living, and live the life they want. At least I think that's my specialty. I haven't coached anyone yet. Maybe I'm special at something else.

KATE: And…what qualifications do you have?

LEAF: The certificate.

KATE: Right, right. But…like…what about your life…in your treehouse…makes you feel that you are qualified to tell other people how to live?

(LEAF *sits next to* KATE *on the couch, takes her hands in his, and looks deeply into her eyes.*)

LEAF: I'm getting a real sense of judgement from you, Kate.

KATE: No, no! I just…I don't know anything about life coaching. I'm curious.

LEAF: I have experience following my dreams and living the life I want, and I want to help others do that too. (*He leans back to drink his soda, and spills it down his front.*)

KATE: So…you're living your dreams. Right now.

LEAF: Oh, yeah. I've come a long way since New Hampshire, baby.

KATE: Oh, I love New Hampshire! What part?

LEAF: Hanover. And my parents wanted me to go into finance, and I just did what they said. Went to the local college in town, and like halfway through had a breakdown. Universities are soul crushers.

KATE: I teach at a university.

LEAF: I know that.

(*Beat*)

KATE: (*Teasing*) I'm getting a real sense of judgment from you, Leaf.

(*Beat*)

LEAF: Anyway, I didn't know how to get out. And I was like, "Dude, this can't be the next forty years of my life; just getting rich and being sad". That's when I went to Guatemala.

KATE: To become Lance Armstrong.

LEAF: Right. And while I was there, I was like, happy. Like, there's this African Gray parrot that hangs out at my treehouse sometimes. He can talk, and those birds are like, thousands of dollars. So he definitely belongs to someone. But I'm not taking him back. I'm not shoving him back in his cage. We're free, and we're never going back.

KATE: What did your parents think about your new, uncaged life?

(LEAF *gets up and starts putting on his jacket.*)

LEAF: I don't know. I haven't talked to them since I left for Guatemala.

KATE: When you were in college?!

LEAF: Yep. I'm a free bird. Like a runaway parrot. *(He zips his coat.)* Cool. Well, I'll be back tomorrow to rip out your bathtub.

(LEAF *turns to leave, and* BEN *walks in the door as he does.*)

BEN: Hi, man!

(LEAF *high fives him and pulls a book out of his backpack.*)

LEAF: Hey! Here's that bird book I told you about! See you tomorrow! *(He exits.)*

BEN: Tomorrow? Why is he coming back tomorrow?!

KATE: *(Hopping over the couch)* He has to rip out the bathtub. It's free, it's fine. Why is he giving you a book?

BEN: It's a bird book. I fell into this youtube spiral about birdwatching. You can get this app that's a bird checklist, and try to mark off all the birds you see. Hey, you'd like this--there's even a birdwatching code of ethics!

KATE: Yikes. How deep was that spiral?

BEN: Most of Wednesday night.

KATE: What about the rocks?

BEN: I can do both! Look down, there's a rock. Look up, there's a bird. Look straight, there's my wife.

(BEN *kisses* KATE.)

KATE: Well, that's…great. Hey, get this. I think Leaf went to Dartmouth!

BEN: What? Get out.

KATE: He said he went to the local college in Hanover, New Hampshire? That's Dartmouth! And he's a life coach!

BEN: What are you, BFFs now?

KATE: Leaf. Is a life coach. I need you to be as confused by this as I am.

BEN: Meh. Literally anyone can become a life coach. I looked into it once.

KATE: You did?

BEN: After a bad day of work. Trying to figure out what else I could do in this town besides help people who packed their laptop in their suitcase and had shampoo leak all over it.

KATE: *(Teasing)* Or watch birds?

BEN: Yeah. *(Beat)* Zach called today. He said there's an opening for a senior engineer in his company. Said I should apply for it.

KATE: In…California?

BEN: Yeah. *(Beat)* I know it's far. And like, your position…

KATE: Yeah…I can't really leave. I'm tenure track.

BEN: There's a lot of universities in California.

KATE: Right, but tenure doesn't always transfer. And these jobs are impossible to get. I know a guy who was full time at NYU, and moved out here for his wife's job, and he's never been full time again anywhere. In twenty-five years.

BEN: Yeah. I get that. It's just…there's nowhere to do what I do in this town.

KATE: We've talked about this. There are plenty of places. It's a big town.

BEN: We *have* talked about this. The only jobs available here are for junior engineers. That's like, 50K.

KATE: Well, that's more than you're making at Best Buy.

BEN: *(With distain)* It's not even about that. I was a senior project manager, Kate. I was making three times that. I'm not going to go be a junior engineer for some guy younger than me.

KATE: Look, babe, I know it sucks, but you might have to work your way back up again.

BEN: But I wouldn't if I went to work for Zach. *(Beat)* It's just—the fact that I *know* someone there, who reached out to me—I actually have a real shot at this job. That might never come around again. *(Beat. He throws up his hands in pretend surrender.)* Let's talk about something else.

KATE: Let's. *(Beat)* Oh, guess what? Remember Mitchell?

BEN: Was that the weird kid that kept bringing his typewriter to our house?

KATE: Yes! He came by my office today and told me he got into grad school! Columbia! How amazing is that?!

BEN: That's great!

KATE: It's unbelievable! I spent hours—*hours*—working with him.

BEN: I remember. The smell of the white-out is burned into my brain.

KATE: He could barely write when I met him, and now he's going to grad school! I'm just over the moon for him. I almost exploded when he told me!

BEN: Aww, good for Mitchell! I feel like I contributed in a small way, for the pots and pots of coffee I made you two while you were working on his thesis. Back when I was learning how to roast beans and make foam art and stuff.

(KATE *hugs* BEN *playfully.*)

KATE: You sustained us!

BEN: Is it weird that I feel like...proud of him?

KATE: No! I'm so proud of him I could burst.

BEN: Man, if we feel this proud of strange little Mitchell, imagine how it will feel when it's our kid getting into grad school!

KATE: I know, right?

BEN: *(Playfully)* Well, we should get on that. What's the date? Is it an ovulation day?

(KATE *sighs.*)

KATE: Wow. That is like your superpower.

BEN: What?

KATE: To somehow turn every topic of conversation to ovulation. Can we please take one night off from this?

BEN: We take plenty of nights off from—

KATE: I know, Ben. But like, somehow in the last couple of years we went from being these cool people that like, travelled and watched documentaries and had dinner parties and had sex just because we felt like it to...I don't know, these weird maniacs who only talk about mucus temperatures. Would you be friends with us? I wouldn't be friends with us.

BEN: Oh my God, Kate, I'm trying to… *(He stops himself.)*

KATE: What?

BEN: Nothing.

KATE: No, what?

(BEN sighs.)

BEN: Look. I'm like, a modern, progressive guy, right? I cook. I do dishes.

KATE: You exfoliate.

BEN: We're not telling people about that one. But I…I don't know. You're doing this awesome work with your students. I have this menial job. I'm not providing. I can't get my wife pregnant. And it's so stupid, but it's like…I don't feel like a man, or something. And then I feel like a caveman for feeling that way, but…I can't help it.

(KATE takes BEN's face in her hands.)

KATE: You are the best man in the whole world. None of that stuff matters.

BEN: Except it does. We say it doesn't, but it does. And if it's an ovulation day we don't want to miss—

(KATE stops BEN.)

KATE: I know. I get it. I just…I miss us.

BEN: I miss us too. *(Beat)* Should we have Secret Hour?

KATE: Yes, yes, yes! Oh my God, we haven't done that in a long time. It always makes me feel better!

BEN: I don't know why. It's a humiliating game.

KATE: But after you humiliate yourself, you get the comfort of knowing you are loved and accepted for exactly who you are, no matter what. Let's play!

BEN: Very well. *(He leans back and pretends to light a cigarette; very dapper.)* Tell me a terrible secret.

KATE: *(She laughs.)* Um—

BEN: Just so you know, I have kept all of your previous secrets. Including that you once made up a fake language to get out of talking to a telemarketer, that you have pulled a hair from your own head to use as dental floss before an important meeting—

KATE: Forgot I told you that one.

BEN: —and that though you pretend to hate it, you cry every time you hear The Christmas Shoes.

KATE: His mom is gonna die! On Christmas!

BEN: And so now, in this baby-free zone, tell me a new secret.

(Beat)

KATE: Baby-free zone, huh?

BEN: As you requested.

(Beat)

KATE: Ok…um… *(She thinks a long time; she seems nervous; really considering. Something shifts, an idea is discarded. Finally she speaks.)* I think three-legged dogs are creepy as hell. And I know people adopt them and my heart is supposed to be warmed and I'm supposed to be so happy that that dog is having a good three-legged life, but it makes my stomach flop to watch them tripod around with an empty spot where a leg should be. *(She playfully hides her face behind her hands.)* I'm pretty sure that makes me a terrible person.

BEN: *(Also playfully)* You're a monster.

KATE: I know!

BEN: You're a *monster*! Who hates three-legged dogs?!

KATE: I do! It's my terrible secret and we're married and you already promised to love me forever, so now you have to take it to your grave.

BEN: Oof. That was a rough one.

KATE: Okay, your turn.

BEN: I don't have any secrets.

KATE: Oh, no you don't. You don't get to judge me and then not share one! *(She playfully crawls across the couch to him.)* I just know you have a deep, dark, terrible secret you want to get off your chest.

(KATE laughs, BEN smiles. A long moment that somehow becomes incredibly uncomfortable. She backs away a little. Silence)

BEN: I do.

(Another long moment.)

KATE: *(Apprehensively)* What is it?

(Beat. We see a similar shift in him that we saw in KATE, where an idea is discarded and another is picked up.)

BEN: Until like, three months ago…I didn't know about the word "wreath".

(Beat)

KATE: What?

BEN: I thought it was reef, and it was two things. Like, the great barrier reef, and a Christmas reef.

KATE: You're kidding.

BEN: I swear to you.

KATE: You're married to a *teacher*! That is so much worse than mine. I'm telling everyone.

BEN: You can't. You have to accept me as I am, secrets and all. Those are the rules of Secret Hour, and they are written in stone.

KATE: Well, there we have it. I'm a monster, and you're...an idiot.

(BEN *laughs*.)

BEN: Monster and Idiot, together forever.

(BEN *pulls* KATE *close and kisses her. She stands up and crosses left, and she is back in her lecture hall. He remains on the couch. Transition to—*)

Scene Three

(*About a month later. March. A split scene.* KATE *is back in her lecture hall, teaching a class.* BEN *is at home, splitting his time between frantically typing on a laptop, and texting furiously on his phone.*)

KATE: So, before we head off on spring break, we will focus on the Confucian side of our argument. Contrary to what many of you wrote on your pretests at the beginning of the semester, he is not— (*She reads from a student's paper.*) "The dude who writes fortune cookies". Fun fact, while Confucius is from China, fortune cookies are not. They started in San Francisco. Confucius, our Chinese philosopher, says that your highest ethical calling is to your family and society. His big idea is the concept of "ren". No Stimpy. "Ren" means humanity, and in Chinese, the literal translation is "two persons in relation". (*She glances at a particular audience member as a "student".*) Get your mind out of the gutter, Mr Stanley. He means that we are only truly human when in relation to other people, fulfilling our roles in society. (*Beat*) Those might be the roles of a parent, a colleague, a daughter, a spouse. A part-time pizza delivery guy, in Mr Stanley's case.

Here's the kicker. Let's say you are a parent caring for a child. That role requires patience, care, selflessness. Confucius says you can't just go through the motions— you have to actually *feel* those things. And he says people who don't lack virtue. They remain self- interested and egotistical; trapped in themselves. You go from being "ren" to being "xiaoren", which means a "small, petty, or diminished person". *(Beat)* That's not to say you can't learn virtue—both Aristotle and Confucius agreed on this. They also agreed that the best way to do this is to mirror virtuous people— identify people around you who genuinely inspire you to live a better life, and then try your best to model what they do. They are your "Polestar", as Confucius says. So on these index cards, I would like you to write down your Polestar for the second half of the semester.

(KATE starts to hand out index cards, and the focus shifts to BEN on the other side of the stage, in their house. He works on a laptop. LEAF enters from the bathroom and stands behind him for a moment, observing the laptop.)

LEAF: Hey, man!

(BEN, startled, snaps his laptop shut.)

BEN: God, Leaf! How long have you been standing there?

LEAF: *(Looking at his watch)* Fifteen seconds? But like, what is time?

(BEN and LEAF look at each other for a moment. LEAF exits into the kitchen. Focus shifts back to KATE in her lecture hall.)

KATE: Alrighty. Let's see what virtuous people we will be mirroring this semester. *(She reads off of the notecards.)* "Buddha." Good choice. "Martin Luther King Jr." "Ghandi." "Jesus." You guys really go for it, huh? Good luck. Oh, here we go. "My dad." I'm just gonna trust you on that one. *(She flips to a new card.)* "Professor Gordon." *(She squints to read tiny writing on it.)* "I swear I'm not sucking up, I find you very inspiring and you are my polestar." *(A long moment as she considers this. It makes her uncomfortable, which she of course covers with a joke.)* Better hope that's not a lie or you're doubly screwed, am I right? Alright, that's all for today. I'll see you after break!

(Lights down on KATE. *Focus shifts back to* BEN. *His phone rings.)*

BEN: Hello? *(Beat)* Yes, this is he. *(He listens.)* Oh, my God. Is she okay? *(He listens. His panic is rising.)* Oh, God, oh God. Saint Mark's Hospital? I'm coming. I'll be there right now. I'm on my way. *(He grabs his coat and races out the door.)*

Scene Four

(Later that day. A waiting room at Saint Mark's Hospital. BEN *sits anxiously—bouncing his foot, wringing his hands. Hospital sounds of doctors being paged, etc. A doctor comes out.)*

DOCTOR: Kate Gordon?

*(*BEN *leaps to his feet.)*

BEN: Yes! Yes, how is she?

DOCTOR: Your wife's going to be fine. She had some small internal injuries—she's just coming out of surgery. She's a little banged up, but she'll be ok. She was talking with us just fine before she went under though. Not everyone has a sense of humor in the ER. She's funny.

*(*BEN's *face crumples.)*

BEN: Yeah, she is. She's amazing. Thank you for helping her.

DOCTOR: Have you been in here before? Did I treat you for cake cramps?

BEN: Was it a bad accident? Was anyone else hurt?

DOCTOR: My understanding was she was the only car involved. Went off the road and hit a tree.

(Beat)

BEN: Wh—why would that happen?

DOCTOR: Could be a number of reasons. Animal ran out in front of her. Maybe she fell asleep or passed out at the wheel. Can happen when you're under stress.

BEN: *(Sighing)* Yeah, we've been under some stress—

DOCTOR: She'll be a little loopy for a bit, but you can go in and see her soon. Oh, also she kept asking about this before she went under, but you can let her know we were able to replace her IUD.

(A long beat)

BEN: *(Dumbfounded)* She was drunk?

DOCTOR: No, that's a DUI. IUD. Birth control. It's very rare that an accident like this could jolt it loose, but we got it replaced.

BEN: That can't be right. We've been trying to have a baby forever. How could she be taking birth control?

DOCTOR: Oh. Um…you don't take it. It's an intrauterine device. *(He holds his fingers about an inch apart.)* It's about this big. Inserted into the uterus. It's on her chart.

(Beat)

BEN: Maybe…maybe she didn't know she had one?

DOCTOR: …Definitely not.

(BEN sinks to sit in a chair in disbelief.)

DOCTOR: Look…the good news is, she's ok, and she should be awake in just a little bit. You can go see her.

(The DOCTOR *leaves.* BEN *sits in silence.)*

Scene Five

(Later that day. KATE's *hospital room. She sleeps,* BEN *paces back and forth near the foot of her bed. The rhythmic beeping of a heart monitor fills the silence. After a while, she stirs and starts to wake up. She sees him—it's clear she's pretty drugged up.)*

KATE: Hiiiiiiiiiii!

BEN: Hi.

KATE: I'd come hug you, but I'm, ya know, tethered to this bed.

BEN: Right. Sorry.

*(*BEN *crosses and kisses* KATE *on the cheek.)*

KATE: You okay?

BEN: Mmm-hmm. How are you feeling?

KATE: Pretty good, actually. Whatever they've got me on is niiiice. *(She looks down and sees the bandages on her arm. She is really drugged out.)* Oh, man. That's gonna be ugly. You should see the other guy, though.

BEN: The tree?

(Beat)

KATE: Is that what I hit?

BEN: Yup.

KATE: I definitely win then. I'll be better in a few months. It's gonna take that tree years to go back to normal. Kate one, Tree zerooooooooooooooo!

(KATE *holds up her good hand to high-five.* BEN *doesn't take the bait.*)

BEN: Yeah, what happened there?

(*Beat.* KATE *starts picking things up from her bedside stand, and turning them upside down, one by one, as she talks.*)

KATE: You know, I don't know. I remember getting in my car after class. I remember driving, and then…I woke up here. I don't know.

(*The last thing is a cup of water, which* KATE *picks up to turn upside down, but* BEN *swoops in and takes it. He sits on a chair next to the bed, quiet and mulling.*)

KATE: You're cranky. Want me to turn you upside down?

(BEN *doesn't answer.* KATE *uses a goofy voice.*)

KATE: Come on! Talk to me!

BEN: I can't talk to you right now; you're all drugged out.

(KATE *picks up a spoon from the side table.*)

KATE: I know! Maybe you should talk to Mrs Spoon! Here, I'll show you. (*She turns to face the spoon*) Mrs Spoon, I don't know what I'm on, but I feel like, free. Like, really free.

(*Beat*)

BEN: Yeah? Maybe we should play a game.

KATE: Okay. Like Uno?

BEN: No. I want to play Secret Hour. (*Beat*) You go first.

KATE: Okay! I have a really good one. You'd never guess it!

BEN: Let's see.

KATE: (*Starting to laugh uncontrollably*) It's so good! It's so good! I didn't know that wolverines are real animals. I thought it was just one of the X-men. *(Beat)* I think if they had called him Wolverine-Man I would have pieced it together. There's Batman and Spider-Man, and bats and spiders are real. Wolverine-Man would have really helped me out. *(She keeps laughing, and almost in the same breath—)* Oh! Also, I'm on birth control.

(KATE lets out a huge sigh. BEN is a little taken aback—he knew it, but didn't expect it to come out like this. A little aggressive.)

BEN: How long?

KATE: Woah, hey, calm it down. You're scaring Mrs Spoon. How long, Mrs Spoon? *(She makes the spoon whisper in her ear.)* She says two years.

(BEN laughs in disbelief and sinks into a chair.)

BEN: Two years. Two years. Why?

(KATE doesn't answer.)

BEN: Why would you do something like this?

(Beat. KATE holds up a finger so she can consult with Mrs Spoon, who whispers in her ear. She whispers for a long, long time.)

BEN: Why, Kate?

KATE: Eh, eh, eh.

(KATE shakes the spoon, implying that BEN must address the spoon.)

BEN: I'm not having this conversation with a spoon!

(KATE gasps, turning the spoon back to her.)

KATE: *(To the spoon)* I am so sorry! He is so rude!

BEN: I can't do this right now. *(He turns to leave.)*

KATE: *(As the spoon)* There's lots of reasons.

(Beat. BEN turns back. Spoon monologue)

KATE: Did you know when her friend Michelle had her baby, she said her vagina got ripped to shreds? She had to wear a diaper—like, a literal diaper—for months! And your boobs are never the same. Your nipples will point STRAIGHT DOWN for the rest of your life! Like a cow! You become just a giant, diaper cow! Moooooooo!

(BEN *is so disturbed he addresses the spoon directly*)

BEN: Stop! Please stop!

KATE: *(As spoon)* OH, I'M SORRY, IS IT HARD TO *HEAR* ABOUT?!

BEN: This is why she doesn't want to have a baby?!

KATE: *(As spoon)* No! This is all irrelevant! She just heard about it once and can't stop thinking about it!

BEN: Well then, why?! If none of that's the reason, why?

(*Beat.* KATE *is exhausted. She leans back on the hospital bed, covering her face with one arm. A moment. Keeping her face covered, she lifts the spoon one more time—but uses her own voice.*)

KATE: She doesn't want to be a mom.

Scene Six

(*The next day.* KATE *and* BEN *enter their home, coming back from the hospital. It is quiet, somber. He carries her things. She enters and sits on the couch, quietly, looking at her bandaged arm. He takes the bags back to the bedroom, comes back out, regards her on the couch, and goes to the kitchen.*)

BEN: I'm getting a drink. *(Beat)* I haven't had a drink in two years, because I was afraid it would slow down my sperm. Tonight, I am having a drink. (*He pours his drink.*) So. Are we going to talk about it?

KATE: The spoon conversation didn't do it for you?

BEN: Don't make jokes, Kate. I know that's your thing. But I can't, tonight. I just…I can't. Talk to me.

(A long beat)

KATE: Remember you promised to love me forever and accept me exactly as I am.

BEN: I'm not really sure that's on the table right now. I'm going to need a lot of answers. *Why?*

KATE: I don't want to have kids. And it's not because of like, issues with my mother, or trauma from my childhood, or anything else people try to pin it on. That's just how I feel about it. Some people just…don't want kids. I shouldn't have to justify it any more than that. I just…don't.

BEN: Why wouldn't you tell me that?

KATE: I did! I did tell you that! I told you that when we met. I told you that when we got married. And you said that's what you wanted too.

BEN: But then we changed our minds!

KATE: No, *you* changed your mind. After you got fi— *(She cuts herself off. A moment)* And when you told me you changed your mind, I told you I hadn't. But you became obsessed. And I could see it taking priority. Over me. Over everything. And I got scared. And I handled it badly. Really badly. I know that. But…I was so afraid of losing you. I *am* so afraid of losing you. People get divorced over this all the time.

BEN: So divorce me!

KATE: I don't want to divorce you! I love you! I love our life! Why do I have to lose that? *(Beat)* Would you want to lose that?

(BEN doesn't answer.)

KATE: Why does this person who doesn't even exist yet matter more than me? Me, and the life we've built *together*? Where we surprise each other at work with coffee because we stayed up too late the night before watching murder documentaries. Where we...order in brunch on Sundays and eat it in our pajamas. Where we forget to go camping until it's too late every year— and then complain all night because it's forty degrees.

(This elicits the smallest smile from BEN.)

KATE: We've spent eight years building this.

BEN: I don't know, Kate. *(He sighs.)* I'm just...I'm trying to wrap my head around this. Let me get this straight. We had all those talks, and you told me you wanted to have kids. Then you went and got this...this...

KATE: IUD.

BEN: ...that would ensure we *wouldn't* have kids. And then you pretended to be surprised and disappointed every month when you weren't pregnant...for two years. *(Beat)* You really are a monster, you know that?

KATE: I know how it sounds. I didn't feel like I had a choice. I—

BEN: Really? Because it sounds like you were making a choice, every second of every day, to lie to me. Over and over. Millions of times. Forget the fact that you did like, an *insane* thing—the layers of betrayal and deception here are unbelievable! And what? You just hoped I'd never find out?

KATE: I...I knew if I kept telling you how I really felt you would probably leave me for someone else. But if I tried to have kids...and couldn't...you would stay. And eventually I'd be too old and it would just be...off the table.

(BEN is silent.)

BEN: I want to be a father, Kate. I can feel it deep down in the core of who I am. You only get one life, and this is what I want with it. *(Beat)* I want you too, but if you don't want this…they call it a deal breaker for a reason.

KATE: That isn't fair. You changed the rules on me.

BEN: There aren't rules; it's life! It's being a human being. Changed the rules? You changed personalities. I don't even know who the hell you are.

(Beat)

KATE: Yes, you do. You know everything about me. You know all my secrets. I mean, now you really, truly know all of my terrible secrets. There are none left. And I know yours.

(BEN *shifts.*)

KATE: And you know that I am a sane, rational person. And believe me, I am sane and rational enough to know how batshit crazy this all sounds. But you know me. *(She starts to break.)* You know me, Ben. How desperate, and terrified, and…cornered must I have felt to do something like this? *Me?* I didn't know how else to keep you.

(BEN *breaks too. This makes sense.* LEAF *pops his head around the corner.)*

LEAF: Don't break up, you guys.

(KATE *and* BEN *jump.)*

BEN: Leaf! God! *(He stands up and gets his coat.)* I'm going for a walk.

KATE: *(Calling after him)* Ben!

(BEN *exits. A moment.* KATE *curls up in a ball on the couch, numb.)*

LEAF: I've got some good news and some bad news.

KATE: I don't want to hear any news, Leaf. Just do what you have to do and please go home.

LEAF: Okay. The good news was I was at the hardware store and saw a dimmer just like your busted one on the wall here. So I got it. Want me to fix it? Since I'm here?

KATE: I don't care.

(LEAF *walks over to the wall and starts fixing the dimmer.*)

LEAF: The bad news is I've never fixed a dimmer before, so—

KATE: You heard all that?

LEAF: Some of it. But only because I was standing behind the wall, listening. *(Beat)* If it helps, I've never thought you were a monster. And I knew.

KATE: Knew what?

LEAF: That you weren't trying to get pregnant.

(KATE *sits up on the couch.*)

KATE: What do you mean you knew?

LEAF: There weren't any pregnancy tests in the trash. You know, that day you told Ben you took one before he got home.

KATE: You look through our trash?

LEAF: Plus the wine. You always drink wine before he gets home. Can't drink when you're trying to get pregnant.

(*A long moment.* KATE *lays back down in a ball on the couch.*)

KATE: Why didn't you say anything?

(LEAF *comes over and covers* KATE *with a blanket.*)

LEAF: I have to keep my professional boundaries.

KATE: And you don't think I'm a monster?

LEAF: I'm sure you had your reasons.

(LEAF returns to fixing the dimmer. KATE mulls this over. Beat)

KATE: It just seems like…when you have kids…you aren't the protagonist of your life anymore. *(Beat)* And maybe that makes me small. And petty. And incomplete. "Xiaoren." *(She rolls to lay flat on the couch. It looks suspiciously like a therapy session.)* I…I don't have that pull. Whatever that pull is that makes women want to be mothers. *(Beat)* Except when I do. I don't know. I look at some of my friends, and how they've lost every thread of who they were in a sea of vomit and Peppa Pig, and I'm like, God, I don't want that. But then I'll see a mom pushing her daughter on the swings, or cuddling and reading a book, and I'm like, "Well, I do want *that*". There is something that aches inside of me when I see that. And maybe that's the pull. I don't know. It's messy, and complicated, and confusing, and has this crushing deadline where you have to make this massive decision for which you are incredibly uninformed. And it's not like you can take it for a test drive and see how you feel about it. The test drive is the rest of your life.

LEAF: *(Holding a screw in his mouth as he works)* And how does that make you feel?

KATE: Terrified. And liberated. And like I'm missing out. *(A moment)* Maybe I'm going to wake up when I'm fifty and realize not having kids was a huge mistake. Or maybe I'll wake up with my baby one night and realize *that* was a huge mistake. I couldn't do that to a kid—life is hard enough without having a mom who doesn't want to be a mom. *(She thinks.)* I wrote a book on philosophy before we came here. I have five more books inside of me. And I love teaching. Like, I *love* it. So many of the women I know who had goals and

dreams like mine got sidetracked or slowed down
when they had kids, and I'm *so afraid* of losing the
thing that makes me come alive, you know? And I
know for some women, having kids is the thing that
makes them come alive, but I don't know if that will be
me. I don't *know. (A moment)* Except I do know. *(Beat)* I
don't think Ben can ever forgive me. And he shouldn't.

LEAF: He might.

(LEAF turns the light on and off with the dimmer.)

LEAF: Hey! Whaddaya know! Want it on or off?

(Beat)

KATE: On.

(A moment)

LEAF: It's gonna be okay. I'll see you tomorrow.

*(LEAF exits, and the scene transitions around KATE, back to
her lecture hall.)*

Scene Seven

*(KATE steps forward from the couch, and is in front of her
classroom. She is not the funny, bubbly professor from
previous scenes. She is a little broken, subdued. She stands
silently in front of them for a long time.)*

KATE: When I started my doctoral program, the first
thing that my professor said, on the first day, is this.
He said, "If you are going to finish this degree…
if you are going to get this PhD…you are going to
have to be selfish. That is the only way it will happen.
Because everyone is going to try to take it from you.
The people who are supportive of you now, on your
first day, are going to start getting irritated when you
don't have as much time for them. Your spouse. Your
kids. Your friends. Unless you are incredibly selfish

and protective of your dream, you won't achieve it". *(Beat)* I have my PhD. Nietzsche would be proud. *(Beat)* Remember, he thinks that you living an authentic life is the most important thing you can do. Of course, he was a nihilist who believed in personal authenticity over society in order to burn the world down and start a new society with no morals at all. While I wouldn't recommend making Nietzsche your Polestar, he did contribute significantly to thoughts on philosophy and ethics, and his ideas on living an authentic life are worth studying. If you want to study a philosopher who taught authenticity to impact the world for good, you'll have to take Ethics II and learn about Kierkegaard. For now, in Ethics I, we look at Nietzsche and Confucius.

Remember, Confucius told us about filling our roles in society, about becoming ren. Nietzsche has a different idea.

KATE: Socrates, way back, gave us this formula. *(She crosses to a whiteboard and writes "Knowledge = Intelligible = Beauty".)* Knowledge is that which is intelligible, and beauty is a form of knowledge. So for something to be beautiful, it must be intelligible. But Nietzsche says, hey, wait a minute. What about music?

(KATE crosses and clicks a button on a CD player. Beautiful, classical music—something like Debussy's La Catedrale Engloutie—*starts to play under her speech.)*

KATE: People think music is beautiful, but we don't experience music intellectually—we experience the beauty by feeling it. So if beauty is a type of knowledge, and music is beautiful, maybe all knowledge isn't intelligible? *(She erases "intelligible" from the whiteboard, so the equation now reads "Knowledge = Beauty". She starts to pick up steam—it almost starts to feel like a lawyer presenting evidence to a jury to defend her client...herself.)* Nietzsche thinks maybe there's

another type of knowledge—an instinctual knowledge
that's born into us. And that knowledge carries all the
passions and desires that make us who we are at our
core.

So let's think of those desires as a fire. *(She pulls a
lighter out of her pocket, and lights a small flame.)* A well-
controlled flame can fill a whole room with light. But
fire can also be dangerous—it can burn a house down;
take a life. In the same way, our passions can become
violent and dangerous impulses. And so we're taught
to suppress our inner ambitions and desires, and to
use our minds to overcome those passions. *(She closes
the lighter, extinguishing the flame.)* Nietzsche thought
that suppressing our passions is an attack on life itself.
He said that our dreams are what give us the feeling
of being alive, and when we deny them, we imprison
ourselves. We create a battle between our body and our
mind, and when we do that our body turns on itself. It
becomes a place of war.

Instead, Nietzsche thinks that we must allow our fire
to burn brightly. *(She relights the lighter.)* But we have to
learn to harness it.

Think of it as a hot air balloon—our instincts and
passions are the fire, and our intellect is the fabric of
the balloon—and the two work in harmony to fly. This
combination allows us to reach our highest capabilities,
and give the world what we, uniquely, have to give.

Let's be real. Achieving or creating anything
worthwhile in the world is hard. It's really hard. And
we're going to need that inner fire, that passion and
energy, to help us overcome the hard stuff along
the way. When we shut it down and allow for that
war between our mind and body, we pave the way
for mediocrity. But when we make our instinct and
intellect sail in the same direction, we live an authentic

life. And as Nietzsche would say, "You become what you are".

And is it possible that only in being your authentic self, can you impact the world?

(The lights go dark so that only the flame is illuminated in the darkness. Simultaneously, the flame goes out and the music stops.)

Scene Eight

(Two days later. KATE sits on the couch with her laptop. BEN enters carrying a small suitcase. KATE looks at the suitcase with alarm.)

KATE: Why...do you have a suitcase?

BEN: Listen. I'm going to go away this weekend. I need some space.

KATE: Just this weekend?

BEN: For now. I just...I can't think here.

KATE: Where are you going?

BEN: Michigan. To see my parents. *(He heads for the door, grabbing the suitcase.)*

KATE: Wait, right now?

BEN: I mean, in a minute. My flight's in a couple of hours.

KATE: Whoa. You're like, kind of springing this on me.

BEN: Yeah. Not much fun, is it? *(Beat. He reaches for the door.)*

KATE: Don't you need your coat?

BEN: What?

KATE: Michigan in April? You should bring your heavy winter coat. Your mom texts us twelve times a day about the snow.

BEN: I think it will be ok. I'm gonna load up the car. I'll be back.

(BEN *exits. A moment.* KATE *sits on the couch, a little confused and suspicious.*)

KATE: *(Hollering out)* LEAF! *(Beat)* Leaf, I know you're here! Come out!

(LEAF *appears from the hallway—droopy and dejected.*)

LEAF: Hey, what's up?

KATE: What's the matter?

LEAF: Remember the African Grey parrot? In my tree house? The one that—

KATE: Yes, I remember it.

(LEAF *sits sadly on the couch.*)

LEAF: It ran away.

KATE: Oh…I'm sorry. Birds do that, I guess. Fly the coop.

LEAF: No, I think something is wrong with its wing. Like, it *ran* away. On its little legs. I saw it. *(He shows her with his fingers, walking very fast. His voice wavers.)* And now it's gone.

(KATE *sits on the couch by* LEAF.)

KATE: Well, maybe it went back to its owners. Maybe they'll be really happy to have him back.

LEAF: He doesn't have owners. He has prison guards. You can't own a bird.

KATE: Well, a lot of people own birds.

LEAF: Birds are free. *(Beat)* Though after watching him run away and feeling, like, the indescribable pain of his absence, I'm starting to understand the cage thing a little. *(Beat)* You wanted something?

KATE: I was wondering if you knew where Ben is going?

(LEAF freezes.)

LEAF: Michigan.

KATE: Leaf….

(LEAF stands.)

LEAF: Look, I'm not part of this.

KATE: You *are* part of this. You have made yourself part of everything. Where is he going?

LEAF: I mean, I don't know what *city*, specifically…

(KATE slowly backs LEAF against a wall.)

KATE: Listen to me, I know you know because you know everything about us, you creepy lurker. You have ten seconds to tell me or I swear to God—

LEAF: California. He's going to California.

KATE: I knew it. About the job?

LEAF: Yeah.

KATE: Well. I should have known. Why shouldn't he. After what I did, why wouldn't he leave me and go do what he wants. *(Beat)* Why would he lie about it though?

(Beat)

LEAF: I'm sure he has his reasons.

KATE: Leaf…

LEAF: *(Slowly backing offstage, whispering)* I'm not part of this.

(KATE *thinks for a moment, then exits offstage towards the bedroom.* BEN *enters again, gathering some papers on the table.* KATE *enters with a giant duffle bag.*)

BEN: What is that?

KATE: Your winter gear. I can't let you go to Michigan and not be prepared.

BEN: I'm going to be fine, really.

KATE: No! It's freezing! I packed all your sweaters, your parka, your boots, hats, earmuffs. Even some ski gear in case you decide to hit the slopes.

BEN: I don't want to take all that.

KATE: Let me do this for you. It's the least I can do after the *lie* I told.

(*Beat.* BEN *regards* KATE *for a moment.*)

BEN: Great. I'll put it in the car.

KATE: I can drive you to the airport. Make sure you get it all inside okay.

BEN: No! I'll drive myself.

KATE: Well, I'll miss you. You know what, after you head out I think I'll call Zach, in California.

(BEN *stops in his tracks.*)

BEN: What? Why?

(KATE *pulls out her phone.*)

KATE: Well, it's been so long since you've seen him. And who knows when you'll see him again. I was thinking of inviting him out for a visit. Cheer you up, after everything.

(BEN *and* KATE *regard each other for a moment. She holds up the phone.*)

KATE: Shall I call him?

(*A standoff*)

BEN: What do you know?

KATE: What should I know?

(LEAF *enters quietly behind them, standing on a chair to fix a light in a wall sconce.*)

BEN: Alright. Fine. You're soooo good at keeping your own secrets, and sooooo good at figuring out everyone else's. You win, as always. I'm going to California. About that job. You can hardly blame me.

KATE: No, I don't blame you. If you want to go, go. I just don't understand why you're lying about it.

BEN: Because...I don't even know if I'll get it. And I didn't want to add more drama if it's nothing. It's just an interview.

KATE: Wait...an interview? How do you have an interview already?

(LEAF *whirls around from his chair, speaking in spite of himself.*)

LEAF: It's his third interview. (*He realizes what he's done and turns back to the wall sconce.*)

KATE: What?

BEN: Um...

(LEAF *whirls back around.*)

LEAF: The first two were on the phone. I heard them. Oh my God, I just keep talking. Nothing matters, my bird is gone.

(LEAF *whirls back to the wall.* BEN *crosses to him.*)

BEN: What do you mean you heard them?

LEAF: I was here! You should just assume I'm always here!

BEN: No! We should not assume that! (*He whirls around to* KATE.) Maybe you're right! Maybe we don't need to have a kid! We have one! It's forty years old and it never moved out! *Why are you always here?* Why? Nights, weekends? *Why?*

KATE: Don't yell at him!

LEAF: I'm fixing stuff!

KATE: He knew about me and the IUD too. He knows everything.

BEN: Are you kidding me? Well, we see whose secrets he kept, didn't we?

LEAF: If I can just say, as a life coach—

KATE & BEN: SHUT UP, LEAF.

LEAF: Yup. *(He turns back to the wall sconce.)*

KATE: How is this your third interview? When was the first one? When did you even apply?

BEN & LEAF: January.

(BEN shoots LEAF a look, and LEAF scurries out of the room. KATE sinks to sit on the arm of the couch.)

KATE: January? *Four months ago,* January?

BEN: Yeah.

KATE: But...you just told me about this job. You applied for it before you even told me about it?

(Beat)

BEN: I told you about it when I got the second interview.

KATE: *Second?* Oh, my God!

BEN: I didn't know if it was going to come to anything, and I didn't want to—

KATE: See, I was willing to assume that this was my fault, because you applied after finding out what I did. But it seems these events are...unconnected.

(Beat)

BEN: Yeah.

KATE: And you were going to let me keep thinking it was my fault.

(BEN *shifts uncomfortably.*)

KATE: Are you kidding me, Ben? You've been laying it on about what a horrible person I am, and what a terrible thing I've done, when you were doing the exact same thing?

BEN: Whoa, whoa. These are not the same *at all.*

KATE: They're lies, Ben! Lies to each other about our future!

BEN: Don't act like what I did was as bad as what you did! You kept us from having a family. I applied for a job.

KATE: Behind my back! And it's a job that would tank everything I've been working for, and you knew that! What was your plan if you got it?

BEN: Well, then I'd have to try to talk you into what I wanted! Just like you were going to *dupe* me into what you wanted.

KATE: Don't give them different labels! It's the same thing.

BEN: No, because mine was going to be a conversation—

KATE: After you already had the job? That's not a conversation—we already *had* the conversation and you just didn't like how it went and barreled on ahead anyway—

BEN: —and yours was going to be an "omission of the truth" until I could never have a family.

KATE: You have a family. You *have* a family! *This* is the family we agreed to!

BEN: Well, then my *family* just sat there and watched me not have kids, hate my job, hate this town. I'm *drowning* here, Kate—my God, you watched me reach for anything—*anything*—to buoy me up and give me something to hold on to! Rock collecting? Roasting coffee? Bird watching?! I mean, thank God that IUD worked, right, because you would be a shit mother. *(Beat. He can sense that that was too far, but holds his ground.)*

KATE: You want to play that game? How about this. It's your own fault you hate your life now, because you got yourself fired. And I'm tired of dancing around it for your ego.

BEN: You know that—

KATE: *You* made a *series of choices*—including some lies—that got you fired. But you know what? Maybe you wouldn't have had to tell those lies if you were a good engineer. *(A moment. She can sense that she, too, maybe went too far, but decides to barrel on ahead.)* You didn't ever seem to care that much about having a baby until you lost your job.

BEN: That's not true.

KATE: It's like you had to replace your identity with *something*, and picked a baby. You're always just floundering around, looking for the world to slap a label on you and tell you who you are. "Well, if I can't be an engineer, I'll be a rock collector. I'll be a bird watcher. I'll be a dad." That's not a good enough reason to have a baby, and it's sure as hell not a good enough reason to turn my life upside down too.

BEN: Don't tell me how I feel, or what I want. Especially while you're over here with your identity so wrapped up in your job that you'll detonate your whole life to protect it! And mine too!

KATE: Oh, I'm sorry, I seem to remember that getting *my* job is the thing that saved us when we were left with nothing. And I didn't even want to teach, Ben! I was doing this for us! But you know what? Along the way, I found out that I *love* it and I'm *good* at it, and I have a future in it. And I'm sorry it's not in New York or California, but this is where I got hired.

BEN: Yeah, I guess they save the good teaching jobs for people who actually sold copies of their books.

KATE: I'm busting my butt for us, and you want me to have a baby *and* bring home a salary while you dick around at Best Buy.

BEN: I am offering a solution! We go to California! I make the money! You can go back to writing your little books and I'll support you *and* a baby.

KATE: That. Right there. The fact that you can call them my "little books" shows that *you don't get it.* You're right—you don't know who I am.

BEN: What do you want, Kate? This is a good life I'm offering—it's the life everybody wants! And you act like I'm some kind of villain for offering it!

KATE: You aren't offering it, you're forcing me into it. And no, that isn't the life I want, and you know that. I cannot just be tossed around in Tornado Ben, being thrown all over the country whenever you get hired or fired, with no regard for my life or my feelings or my dreams!

BEN: If you want to have a conversation about regarding other people's lives, and feelings, and dreams, I am *happy* to have that conversation with you. I would *love* to have that conversation with you, Kate. I would love to hear your thoughts on that topic, and on putting yourself first. But I have a plane to catch.

(BEN *gathers up his papers and heads for the door. A moment. Transition begins—*KATE *makes a circle around the couch, gathering papers and her bag and putting on a jacket, which she misbuttons, and putting up her hair in a messy ponytail. Her circle continues to the front of the stage as she enters her classroom and the living room clears away.*)

Scene Nine

(KATE *enters her classroom, completely disheveled and pissed, dropping papers everywhere.*)

KATE: Class has started, everyone shut up. Shut up, Mr Stanley. Yes, you will get your papers back today. You can pick them up off the floor here at the end of class. To be honest, I am offended that I spent so much more time grading them than you clearly spent writing them.

What are we talking about today? *(She flips through her syllabus.)* Ah, back to our old friends, Confucius and Nietzsche. Two dead *men* telling the rest of us how to live our lives. There are women philosophers we'll be looking at later in the semester, but they don't get as much street cred in Intro to Ethics, because their ideas aren't as old, because women weren't allowed to have ideas until somewhat recently in history. But I don't think that keeps us from the fact that our friends Confucius and Nietzsche, and their theories on ethics, cannot be separated from gender.

Because let's be real. Traditionally, men are raised to follow a Nietzschean belief in themselves. He was a real misogynist, by the way. He once claimed that women love injustice and are incapable of friendship. Meanwhile, boys are encouraged to value independence, their own rights, disconnection from others. I offer up any superhero movie as evidence. And usually that also includes seeing other people and relationships as roadblocks to becoming all you can be. Pesky Mary Jane and Lois Lane, tearing our hero's attention from the grand things he was born to achieve! "Make something of yourself! Be true to who you are! Reach for the stars!" *Become your authentic self.* Frickin' *Nietzsche.*

Before I get a bunch of angry emails about what a man-hater I am, let's pause. Not all men are privileged. Race, class, socioeconomics all play a part in that. But whatever class a man falls into, the idea of masculinity gets planted, and historically, he is more privileged than the women in that class. And it's even worse for women of color, or women who are trans or people who are non-binary.

Because let's talk about women. *(She pauses, acknowledging a question from a student.)* No, this is not on the syllabus. I am changing the syllabus for today, because this is my class and I'm in charge and I can talk about whatever I want to talk about. *(She looks over at another student's question.)* Is this going to be on the test? Yes, this will be on the test. The test is called *your life.*

So let's talk about women, who are typically shoved into a Confucian destiny. Women—and people with uteruses—are the only ones who can get pregnant and give birth. So it all falls to us. We are the only ones who can fulfil that particular Confucian role in society. Carol Gilligan, a psychologist, did a study and found that women were *just as likely* to express desires towards those Nietzschean ideas as they were to desire relationships—intimacy—caring for others. And yet many had been raised to believe that autonomy is an "illusory and dangerous quest". "You are a wife. You are a mother. That is the highest aspiration you should pursue."

And maybe some of you want to pursue that. For you, that *is* you being your authentic self. And nothing that Nietzsche, or Confucius, or Carol Gilligan or I or anyone else says should ever, ever influence you otherwise.

But it's not always as clear for some of us, is it? (*She looks at her watch.*) Um, we're just about out of time. I wasn't planning on lecturing on this today, so I don't have like, a nice, neat wrap up for you. In fact, I don't think there is one, because the world doesn't have a nice, neat wrap up for you on this topic. But I do think it's worth talking about. If you are pondering the big question—is your highest ethical responsibility to yourself, or to other people—you have to consider how your gender plays into your ideas on who you are and who you are expected to be. (*She tiredly gestures to the papers on the floor.*) Don't forget your papers.

Scene Ten

(*A couple of days later. Back at the apartment.* LEAF *is organizing a box of tools on the dining room table.* BEN *enters with his suitcase. He regards* LEAF *for a moment.*)

BEN: Hey.

LEAF: Hey.

(BEN *crosses and takes his suitcase offstage. He returns.*)

BEN: Look, things got kind of…heated before I left. I'm sorry you got caught in the middle. I said some things I shouldn't have.

(BEN *crosses to the kitchen and gets a beer. He also gets one for* LEAF. *He hands it out to him as a peace offering.*)

LEAF: No, hey man, that's on me. I was, like, all distraught about my parrot. I shouldn't have said anything.

(BEN *opens his beer and sits in a side chair.*)

LEAF: Did you get the job?

BEN: I don't know yet. (*He takes a drink.*) Wasn't my best interview. I was…distracted. Is she here?

LEAF: No. Should be home soon. (*He goes back to his box of tools on the table.*) What kind of job is it? In California?

BEN: Designing security software.

LEAF: Duuuuude. You know how to do that?

BEN: Duuuuude. That's what I used to do before.

LEAF: Why'd you stop?

(BEN *sighs.*)

BEN: I don't know.

LEAF: Sure you do. (*A moment*) Have you seen any blue jays? For your app?

BEN: Oh. I'm not really doing that anymore. I probably saw some in California.

LEAF: You are a terrible bird watcher. They don't live in California. Did you know that blue jays are the most deceptive bird?

BEN: Excuse me?

LEAF: That's what they're known for. They impersonate hawks and scare away all the other birds, and then they get the bird feeders all to themselves. People say they're dicks, but I think they're just trying to survive, you know? Like, sometimes we just lie to survive.

(*Beat*)

BEN: You already know, don't you?

LEAF: Just what I heard when I pressed my ear to the door. What lie got you fired?

(BEN *sighs.*)

BEN: I was designing security software, and it had an error that I missed. It was a dumb error. And rather than tell everyone I'm dumb, I tried to cover it up. Which got more and more complicated. And of course when the program failed they eventually traced back all the stuff I did to cover it up, and they fired me. *(Beat)* Crazy thing is if I'd just told them when I discovered it, I would have been in trouble, but I wouldn't have been fired.

LEAF: You do that a lot?

BEN: Make dumb mistakes?

LEAF: Make them worse by trying to cover them up?

BEN: Nope. Stop. Don't try to life coach me. *(Beat)* But yeah, apparently I do that a lot. It's just…I know it's my fault we're here. But do I have to be punished for the rest of my life? I screwed up, I own that, but when do I get to move on? When do I get to be happy again?

(KATE *enters with her teaching stuff. She pauses in the doorway when she sees* BEN.)

BEN: Hey.

KATE: Hey. *(She crosses to the hallway with her stuff. She comes back and sits in the other side chair, so she,* BEN, *and* LEAF *are seated in a triangle.)* I don't know what to say.

BEN: I don't know what to say either.

(Beat)

LEAF: I know what to say.

(BEN *and* KATE *both look at* LEAF.)

LEAF: I think you should play your secret game. *(He widens his arms as if laying an offering on the table for them, then stands up and exits into the hallway.)*

KATE: I don't want to play that now. Look, Ben, I don't—

BEN: *(Cutting her off)* I don't think Meryl Streep is all that.

(KATE gasps.)

KATE: What?!

BEN: That's my secret. She's good, but so are a lot of people. She's just good at raising a slow eyebrow, and it makes everyone feel uneasy, so she seems powerful, so we think she's the greatest. You go.

KATE: Jeez. Um, okay. Once, in high school, I was shopping and my lips were really dry, and I used a lip gloss at the store and then put it back. I didn't buy it. And—

(LEAF bursts out of the hallway, clapping his hands.)

LEAF: Ohhh-KAY! You can't play this game unsupervised anymore because YOU! ARE! LIARS! What is this game?! "Unimportant, Safe Secrets We Tell Each Other While Our Real Secrets Eat Us Up Inside" Hour? Do you ever share anything real? Meryl Streep? Petty crime?! Come on! You have someone to share the deepest parts of who you are with, and you don't do it! You chicken out every time! I have one! I have one! *Your house has been fixed for months.*

KATE: What?

LEAF: Your house has been fixed for months! I fixed the pipe, I replaced the carpet, that was one week. That was it. That's all it needed.

BEN: But what about the tub?

LEAF: Made it up. Wasn't real.

KATE: But…you ripped our bathtub out of the wall.

LEAF: Didn't need to. All for show.

BEN: Why?!

LEAF: Because here's another secret. *I'm lonely as shit,* okay? *That's* how you play Secret Hour. You reveal something real. I win your stupid game.

KATE: But…you're not lonely. You're free! You said you were free and happy.

LEAF: Yeah, you know what comes with being free? Being totally alone. Because as soon as you invite someone else into your life, you aren't free. But I came here and I fixed your pipe—which by the way, took two seconds with a wrench. Learn a skill. Either of you. And like…I don't know. I liked you. I liked talking to you, and eating cake with you. And you have indoor plumbing, which is like, a big deal when you live in a treehouse. *(Beat)* There. Now you know both of my secrets, and I'm your handyman so you have to love and accept me exactly as I am.

BEN: Um…we're actually probably going to have to report you to someone. That is…highly unethical.

LEAF: It's not like I charged you. Now *you* play secret hour, but do it for real.

(BEN *and* KATE *regard each other. She inhales to speak, then looks at* LEAF. *It's weird that he's still here.*)

LEAF: Oh, no. I'm going to sit here because I already know all of your secrets and I'm going to hold you accountable and make sure you don't do any more lip gloss bullshit. Jeez.

KATE: Okay. Um… *(She takes a deep breath. She turns to face* BEN.*)* I do know what happened on the day of my car crash. *(Beat)* I taught that ethics class that day, and one of the students said I was her Polestar.

LEAF: *(In a soothing counselor voice)* Which is....

KATE: ...a person that inspires you to live a better life. And she said I was hers. And I knew I was about as far from being a virtuous person as you can get. And it wasn't even that I felt crushed by the secret, or by the lying. What got me was...it actually really scared me, how good I was at faking it. How no one, not even you, knew who I was. I could fool everyone, for as long as I wanted. And it made me feel like no one would ever really know me, in my whole life. And I felt so, so, so... alone. *(Beat)* And I got in the car to drive home, and I just started crying. I've never cried like that—like, out of control. And I started to drive, thinking I was either going to have to tell you, which would be the end of us, or I was going to have to go on living this lie forever, being unknown and alone, and the weight of both of them felt like this...pressure on my chest. I had a panic attack. I couldn't breathe. I felt like I was dying, and my vision was going dark, and I tried to pull over, but I was starting to black out, and...the tree.

(Beat. LEAF leans over to BEN.)

LEAF: Okay, I actually didn't know that one. *(He leans over and takes KATE's hand.)* That wasn't easy. I'm proud of you. *(He leans over and also takes BEN's hand.)* Ben?

(KATE and BEN pull their hands away.)

BEN: I don't know.

LEAF: Yes you do.

BEN: I...um... *(He looks at KATE.)* It really hurts when you say I only want to have a kid because I got fired, and I'm trying to fill some void. It's not true. I didn't used to want to have kids because my dad was so... you know. I didn't think I could be a good dad. But then remember, before we moved here, when Richard asked me to help him coach his kid's soccer team?

KATE: Yeah. You didn't want to do it.

BEN: I thought maybe I'd have a better chance of getting promoted to his project at work if I knew him outside of work. But...there was this one day, during practice, when we took a snack break. I was sitting in a circle in the grass with these five-year-olds. I was trying to open one of those bananas where the stem just bends, but it doesn't open, and it just turns to mush inside. And this little guy next to me put his hand on mine, really gently and said, "No, Mr Ben, you have to *peel* it". And he mimed peeling a banana, because in his mind I had somehow made it to adulthood without figuring out how to peel a banana, and he was going to teach me how. And then he rested his head on my shoulder, and...something happened inside of me. I can't explain it. I could feel something shift, and...I knew wanted to be a dad more than anything. *(Beat)* I think we've been growing apart for a long time. I've felt it. And maybe some part of me thought that having a baby would help that, too. But I think we're just...becoming different people. And we didn't want to admit it so badly that we've turned into crazy people the last few years.

KATE: I have this lecture on Nietzsche.

LEAF: *(Soothingly)* No one cares about that.

KATE: *(Ignoring him)* About how when you aren't your authentic self...your body and you mind are at war. I've felt that for a long time. I felt that all the way into a tree. I was so afraid of you keeping me from who I want to be. And the whole time you were at war too, because I was keeping you from being who you want to be.

(KATE *and* BEN *look at each other sadly.*)

KATE: I think you're right.

LEAF: Wait, wait, wait. You guys were supposed to like, work it out.

KATE: I don't think so.

LEAF: No, guys, that's the whole thing! If you want to have people in your life, you don't get to have everything exactly like you want all the time! That's the trade off! *(Beat)* Everything in my life is exactly what I want, except for the part where I'm so lonely I had a breakdown over a parrot and hid out in your house for four months just so I'd have someone to talk to. Is that what you want? Do you want to rip out and reinstall a bathtub six times? Because that's what you're choosing.

BEN: That is definitely not what I'm choosing.

KATE: Six times?! Come on, Leaf.

LEAF: *(Starting to panic) You* come on! You guys can't break up!

(BEN *and* KATE *exchange a look, then move over and sit next to* LEAF *on the couch. They each take one of his hands and speak to him like their child.)*

BEN: Leaf, Kate and I care about you very much. But sometimes two people just aren't meant to be together anymore. It's not your fault. You didn't do anything wrong.

KATE: Actually, you did many, many things wrong.

BEN: But that's not why we're splitting up. And don't you think, like…staying in a bad marriage and reinstalling a bathtub aren't your only two options? Like, maybe there's a happy medium? For you too?

(LEAF *considers this and calms a bit.)*

LEAF: You're gonna be a really great dad someday. *(He looks at* KATE.) You're right, you're not very maternal. *(He takes a deep breath.)* Okay. There's just the last bit to finish up then.

KATE: The last bit of what?

LEAF: My session. I have a specific way to wrap up my sessions, since I successfully life coached you through this difficult time.

BEN/KATE: I think I just coached *you*—/Um, I don't think that's what just happened at all—

LEAF: Would you have had this conversation without me?

(BEN *and* KATE *consider this.*)

BEN: Probably eventually.

KATE: Probably with more yelling.

LEAF: You're welcome. I'll invoice you later. And so to conclude my session—

(LEAF *pulls his phone out of his pocket and sets it on the table, setting it to play soothing, yoga-esque music. He grabs two candles from the dining room table and lights them on the coffee table.*)

LEAF: —we choose new names.

KATE: I don't think this is life coaching. I think this is like, a séance.

LEAF: Shhh. We choose new names to symbolize your new lives. My third big secret is—my real name is not Leaf.

BEN: Ya don't say.

LEAF: When I left my old life, I left behind my old name and gave myself a new one. My real name…is Anders.

BEN: Yikes. You *are* from New Hampshire. That's pretty douchey.

LEAF: To be fair, "Leaf" is kind of douchey too. But I chose it because I wanted to be free, like a leaf, blowing in the wind. Seeing the world. (*Beat. Still in his soothing voice.*) I didn't really think about how free leaves that see the world are technically dead because they are no longer attached to anything. A lot of things seem to be coming to light now. Now you choose new names.

KATE/BEN: No, thank you./I'm good.

LEAF: Then I will choose them for you.

KATE: This is really how you end all your sessions?

LEAF: You're my first one, but I'm vibing on this pretty good. I think I'll keep it. *(He turns to BEN.)* You, I will name River, as a reminder that you can always go back and fix your mistakes.

BEN: But rivers can't go backwa—

LEAF: *(To KATE)* And you, I name Chameleon, as a reminder that you don't have to change yourself.

(KATE regards LEAF for a moment. Something about that touches her.)

KATE: Okay.

(LEAF places one candle in front of BEN and one candle in front of KATE.)

LEAF: And when you are ready to step into your new life, blow out the candle of your old life.

(BEN and KATE regard each other with wistful sadness. They watch each other as they each lean forward and blow out their candles. Darkness. A somber moment. An ad cuts off the music and plays from LEAF's phone.)

PHONE VOICE: Tired of listening to ads? Subscribe to Pandora now for an ad free experien—

(LEAF lunges forward and turns off his phone. Beat)

LEAF: *(In the darkness)* That wasn't part of it.

Scene Eleven

(About a month later. KATE *and* BEN*'s living room is filled with moving boxes—it's looking bare.* KATE *is placing items in a moving box.* BEN *enters.)*

BEN: Hey.

KATE: Hey.

BEN: So. Are these mine?

KATE: Yeah, I think that's the last of your stuff.

BEN: Thanks. Sorry, I thought I got it all when I was here last week.

KATE: No worries. Did you get my message? About Leaf?

BEN: Yeah. I think that's a good idea.

KATE: Great. He should be here in a minute; we can tell him then. He fixed the baseboard and the dishwasher. Once he finishes that light switch we'll be good for the new owners.

*(*LEAF *enters from the hallway.)*

LEAF: Bathroom's looking good. I polished up that bathtub to a fine sheen.

KATE: Or, we'll just tell them he comes with the house. Hey, Leaf, we were talking and…we want to pay you for the time you were here… "working" on the house.

LEAF: No, that's okay.

BEN: We appreciate that you cared about us, and that's a long time to not make any money. And you live in a treehouse, so…let us do this.

LEAF: It's really okay. No need.

KATE: We want to make sure you're okay.

LEAF: Guys, I studied finance at Dartmouth.

KATE: *(To* BEN*)* I knew it!

BEN: Yeah, but you didn't graduate.

LEAF: I was there long enough to learn about compounding interest. I have like, two million dollars. I'm good.

(BEN and KATE stare at LEAF, dumbfounded. He crosses to a box.)

LEAF: Does this one go in the "across town" truck, or the "California" truck?

BEN: California.

(LEAF picks up a sharpie and writes "River" across the front of the box, and carries it outside. KATE and BEN regard each other for a moment.)

KATE: So.

BEN: So. *(Beat. He gestures around the house.)* All this for a job I didn't even get.

KATE: You'll find something. You'll have more options out there.

BEN: And you're...gonna do great here. They're lucky to have you. *(Beat)* This feels like one of those occasions when you should make a big speech, but...I don't really know what to say.

KATE: I don't either. I love you.

BEN: I love you too.

(BEN and KATE hug. It's painful.)

KATE: I...um...good luck. With everything. I hope you find the job and the baby and...all of it.

BEN: Thanks. Good luck with tenure. I hope you get it.

(LEAF enters again.)

BEN: Leaf! *(He crosses to shake LEAF's hand.)* It's been an...odd few months with you. In a weird way, I'm going to miss you.

LEAF: I'm gonna miss you too, man. Not in a weird way. In a genuine way. *(He crosses to KATE.)* I'm gonna miss you too.

KATE: Oh, I'll just be across town. I'll call you when something breaks in my new place.

LEAF: Oh, no can do. I won't be here. I'm gonna head back to New Hampshire for a while. See my folks.

KATE: You are?

LEAF: Yeah. I want some people in my life. And you can't be my people anymore. I mean, you're not even each other's people anymore. And I can't just sit around waiting for another parrot to find me. So...I think it's time.

KATE: I'm really happy for you, Leaf.

LEAF: Thanks. I'm happy for you guys too. *(Beat)* Isn't it funny how we all like, swapped? Like, you guys used to be together and I was totally alone, and now thanks to you I'm gonna go find my family, and *you guys* are going to be totally alo—

KATE/BEN: We've got it./Thank you, Leaf.

LEAF: I just think it's funny.

(Beat)

BEN: I should probably hit the road.

KATE: Yeah, me too.

(KATE crosses and picks up her purse. BEN grabs his backpack. They look around sadly, then front with some trepidation. LEAF also faces front.)

BEN: *(With uncertainty)* Ready?

KATE: *(Also with uncertainty)* Ready?

LEAF: *(With joy)* Ready.

(Lights out on all but KATE. *She steps forward, and is back in her classroom.)*

Epilogue

KATE: Happy finals day! You made it. To the last day of ethics class. Let me assure you that no matter how ready you are to be done with this class...you are not more ready than I am.

So—is your highest ethical responsibility to yourself, or to other people?

But before we dive into that—what was my one rule this semester?

Do not lie to me. Some of you didn't follow it. *(She pulls out a piece of paper.)* Mr Folks. You said you were late every Tuesday because soccer practice ran late. Looked into it. There is no soccer practice on Tuesdays. Ya busted. *(She flips to another paper.)* Ms Mackey. You wanted an exemption on the first quiz because the bookstore had run out of textbooks, and you couldn't read the chapter. Bookstore had plenty of textbooks, and records show you had already purchased yours. Ya busted. *(She flips to another paper.)* Mr Stanley. Have you heard of plagiarism scanning software? No? I have. Ya busted. *(Beat)* According to my rule for this class, the three of you automatically fail. You don't even need to take today's final. I'm sure you aren't the only three who lied to me this semester...but you're the ones that got caught. *(Beat)* However. *(Beat)* I was thinking about the final exam question this morning. I've been thinking about it all semester, actually, in and out of this room.

In this case, is my highest ethical responsibility to myself? That I keep my word and uphold my policy and fail you? Or is my highest ethical responsibility

to you—my students? To see you as full, complete
people with lives outside of this room that I may know
nothing about—and that as messy, fragile, complicated
people, you told a lie for reasons which may not make
sense to me? *(Beat)* I'm going to do something I've
never done before. I'm going to leave it up to you.
Only you know *why* you lied. And you are going to
write it into your final exam paper today. I will warn
you—keeping a lie inside of you may not affect your
grade, but it affects your life. It affects who you become
and how you live. *(She holds up her arm.)* I will have
scars for the rest of my life, reminding me of that. So...
answer carefully. *(Aside)* Except for you, Mr Stanley.
Plagiarism is like, a really big deal, and you're going
to have to have a conversation with the dean and are
probably expelled. I'm not sure. *(Beat)* So! Over the
course of this semester, have you been won over by
Nietzsche, and his belief that becoming your authentic
self—who you truly are—is your highest calling?

(As KATE *speaks, lights come up on* BEN *on one side of the
stage. He is unpacking his box that says "River," and pulls
out a Christmas wreath. He reads a note attached to it.)*

BEN: "I thought I'd let you have the reef. Good luck.
Kate." *(He gives it a small smile and sets it aside.)*

KATE: Or, do you side with Confucius, and his belief
that while yes, it is important to become an ethical
person yourself, the way you do that is by fulfilling
your role in society, and who you are in relation to
other people?

(As KATE *speaks, lights come up on* LEAF *on the other side
of the stage. He nervously dials his phone.)*

LEAF: Hey. Um...it's me. It's...Anders.

KATE: I encourage you to give specific examples from
your own life supporting your ideas, and why you
believe what you believe.

*(Lights up on all three—*LEAF, KATE, *and* BEN, *each in their own space.)*

KATE: Your time begins now.

(Blackout)

END OF PLAY